PSE in Focus

money makes sense!

Paul Metcalf

D1549492

Published in 2002 by:
Nelson Thornes Ltd
Delta Place
27 Bath Road
CHELTENHAM
GL53 7TH
United Kingdom

02 03 04 05 06 / 10 9 8 7 6 5 4 3 2 1

A catalogue record for this book is available from the British Library

ISBN 0 7487 6221 3

Illustrations by Bill Piggins
Page make-up by Tech-Set Ltd.

Printed and bound in Croatia by Zrinski

Contents

Introduction

The government's intention to include financial capability as an integral part of the National Curriculum is evidenced in the recently published Framework for Personal, Social and Health Education (PSHE) and Citizenship. Teachers and schools have an important part to play in developing pupils' financial capability and ensuring that they take an active role in relation to money management and financial planning.

This book aims to provide teachers with an interesting and informative approach to money. It starts with a history of money and goes on to develop pupils' understanding of income and expenditure in a way that is specifically geared to their interests and lifestyles. The work links in well with PSHE and citizenship programmes as well as offering cross curricular links to other subject areas including history, geography, mathematics, art, modern foreign languages and English.

The book encourages pupils to make independent and informed decisions about budgeting, spending, saving, and investing as well as making use of credit and obtaining value for money. The layout of chapters introduces and defines each topic as well as providing questions to check understanding. Tasks and investigations provide a useful basis for further development work.

Your comments and feedback on the book and its contents are most welcome.

Paul Metcalf
Author

1 A history of money

What's all this about?

Once upon a time, long, long ago…, goods were exchanged using the barter system. Barter means swapping something that you have and someone else wants, for something that they have and you want.

> So far so good…

Of course barter is a clumsy system. For example, if you want a new pair of shoes and all you have are bags of potatoes to trade, then you are going to have to find a cobbler who wants some potatoes.

> Now that could be difficult.

Unfortunately, if the cobbler wants some leather (to make shoes) then you are going to have to find someone who will exchange their leather for your potatoes so that you can trade the leather for that new pair of shoes.

> Are you still following this?

But how much leather should you exchange for those shoes and how many potatoes should you exchange for the leather?

Not surprisingly, people looked around for standard commodities that everybody would be happy to accept for goods and services. These standard commodities became the first money. They included feathers, beads, stones, shells, salt, rice, whales' teeth and cattle.

People were happy to accept these commodities as money because they were confident that everyone else would accept them too. However, they often had drawbacks – how could you pay half a cow for a new television? And going to the shops with a pocket full of whales' teeth could be a bit uncomfortable.

What does this mean?

How would you like a monetary system based on shells, rice and whales' teeth?

How many shells would you want for a paper round?
What is your computer worth in rice?
How many whales' teeth would you need to get into the cinema?

Many civilisations began to turn to metal as their chosen form of money. Metal was an ideal commodity and many metals (such as gold) were valuable, so everyone was happy to accept them as payment. Another advantage of metal was that it could be made into bars or coins. These were easy to carry around.

The money time line in the UK

Today we think of money as coins and banknotes, and perhaps as cheques, debit cards and credit cards.

The history of money is a long history as the following time line shows.

●	155BC	Coins replace the barter system in Britain. The first coins bear the names of tribal kings and queens.
●	43AD	Emperor Claudius invades Britain and Roman coins are adopted as currency.
	765	King Heabert of Kent mints the first silver penny to be produced in the British Isles.
●	1605	Receipts issued by goldsmiths in London are accepted as early banknotes.
●	1662	For the first time, pennies and farthings are made out of copper by machines.
●	1725	Banknotes of fixed amounts (£20, £30, £40, £50 and £100) are produced.

continued

1965	The first cheque guarantee card in the UK is issued by the National Provincial Group of banks.
1966	Barclays launches the first British credit card, based on BankAmericard (now Visa).
1967	Barclays Bank opens the first cashpoint in Enfield, North London.
1971	Britain abandons pounds, shillings and pence and adopts the new decimal system.
1972	A number of banks launch a rival to the Barclaycard called the Access credit card, which is now part of MasterCard.
1980	Banking over the telephone is piloted leading to the establishment of First Direct as a telephone bank.
1987	The first Visa debit card is issued, it is closely followed by the Switch debit card.
1992	The Maastricht Treaty is signed setting a target date for the creation of a single European currency.
1995	Mondex, a form of electronic purse with the monetary amount being stored on a microchip, is piloted in Swindon.
1996	The first secure transaction over the Internet takes place using the account details on a plastic payment card.
2002	Euro notes and coins go into circulation in countries that have signed up to the European single currency.

What do you know?

1 Write down the cost of the following items:

a hamburger
a computer system
a music CD

in terms of **a)** feathers, **b)** beads, **c)** shells and **d)** salt.

2 What other commodities would you like to see used as money? Why?

3 Here are some coins that we do not use any longer…

- Find out what these coins looked like.
- How much are they worth now?
- Ask an adult what they
  remember about them.

4 Do you think we will still be using money in the future?

Draw a time line (like the one on page 2 and 3) for the next 50 years.

5 Design your own set of coins and notes for the future including a £1000 note.

6 Have you ever thought about what happens to the money in your pocket?

- How far does a coin travel in the space of one year?
- What interesting places has it visited?

Write a page about a day (or week or month) in the life of a 20p piece.

2 Shopping around

What's all this about?

One of the pleasures of shopping is spotting a good bargain – but sometimes it's hard to tell what really is a good bargain.

Two for the Price of One

HALF PRICE

Buy One Get The Second Half Price

25% Extra FREE

20% OFF

Three for The Price of Two

Can you spot the bargain among this lot?
Which offer is the better buy?

A SINGLE PACKET OF CHEWIES @ 32P	*or*	**BULK BUY PACK WITH 4 PACKETS OF CHEWIES @ £1.24**

Buy 1 and get 2nd half price
Lemofizz bottle priced 46p

or

Single
Lemofizz bottle priced 34p

A single writing pad (150 pages) **@ 90p**

or

Economy price writing pad (350 pages) **@ £2.20**

400 ml of Hair Gel *reduced from* **99p to 88p**

or

25% extra free 500 ml of same Hair Gel **priced @99p**

Work it out

Did you spot the bargain?

If you want to work out which is the best buy then you are going to have to use some maths.

The maths is not that difficult … in fact it is just common sense.

To compare the cost you find the cost of one unit.

A SINGLE PACKET OF CHEWIES @ 32P	or	BULK BUY PACK WITH 4 PACKETS OF CHEWIES @ £1.24

For the bulk buy pack, the cost of one packet of Chewies is

£1.24 ÷ 4 = £0.31 or 31p so the bulk buy is better value.

Alternatively, you could work out the cost of four single packets of Chewies.

32p × 4 = £1.28 so the bulk buy is better value.

This method is sometimes known as finding the **unit cost**.

To compare the cost just find the cost of one unit (in this case a single packet of Chewies).

Nowadays, the unit cost is often used to indicate what you must pay for a standard amount of something, for example the cost per packet, per litre or per 100 grams. Unit cost is useful because it allows you to compare costs and work out best value for money.

Buy 1 and get 2nd half price **Lemofizz bottle priced 46p**	or	Single **Lemofizz bottle priced 34p**

Here, we need to work out the actual cost of buying one bottle of Lemofizz and the second bottle half price.

The first bottle costs 46p.
The second bottle costs 23p (as it is half price).
The two bottles together cost 46p + 23p = 69p.
So one bottle costs 69p ÷ 2 = $34\frac{1}{2}$p
So the single bottle is better value.

Alternatively, you could work out the cost of two bottles for both cases.
For the *'Buy 1 and get 2nd half price'* offer:

First bottle costs 46p.
Second bottle costs 23p (as it is half price).
The two bottles together cost 46p + 23p = 69p.
For the single bottle:

First bottle costs 34p.
Second bottle costs 34p (as it is the same price).
The two bottles together cost 34p + 34p = 68p.
So the single bottle is better value.

This work seems quite easy doesn't it!

A single writing pad (150 pages) @ **90p**	or	Economy price writing pad (350 pages) @ **£2.20**

For the single writing pad:

  150 sheets cost 90p.
  So 1 sheet costs 90p ÷ 150 = 0.6p.

For the economy writing pad:

  350 sheets cost £2.20 or 220p.
  So 1 sheet costs 220 ÷ 350 = 0.6285714p.
  So the single writing pad is better value.

Alternatively, you could use a different quantity for the unit cost (such as 50 sheets or 100 sheets).

Reduced price 400 ml of shampoo **reduced from 99p to 88p**	or	*25% extra free* 500 ml of same shampoo **priced @99p**

For the reduced price offer:

  400 ml costs 88p.
  So 100 ml costs 88p ÷ 4 = 22p.

For the '25% extra free' offer:

  500 ml costs 99p.
  So 100 ml costs 99p ÷ 5 = 19.8p.
  So the '25% extra free' offer is better value.

Remember that to compare the cost you just find the cost of one unit. In this case you could find the cost of 1 ml of shampoo. However, the maths is easier if you find the cost of 100 ml. Then you can do the calculation in your head!

A final word… Remember that bulk buying is not always a good idea. After all, you might not want five bottles of shampoo.

What do you know?

1 Which offer is the better buy?

a

| A Munchie Bar priced **35 pence** | **or** | A pack of 4 Munchie Bars priced £1.25 |

b

| Buy 2 and get 3rd Free bottle of cola priced 72p per bottle | **or** | Single bottle of cola priced 52p per bottle |

c

| A box of tissues with 100 tissues priced @ **42p** | **or** | An economy size box of tissues with 250 tissues priced @ **£1.10** |

d

| A box of cornflakes (500 g) priced @ £1.55 | **or** | A small box of cornflakes (125 g) priced @ £0.40 |

2 We have already said that you might not want to buy in bulk to get the best value for money. Write down three other reasons for not wanting to buy in bulk?

3 Supermarkets often claim that their typical shopping basket is cheaper than that of their nearest rival.

- List 20 items you think should be in a typical shopping basket.
- Compare the price of your typical shopping basket in two different supermarkets close to you. Which is the better value and why?
- Compare the prices of your typical shopping basket in your local corner shop and at a supermarket. Which is the better value and why? (Remember that you might need to take transport costs into account.)

> Remember that you do not have to go to the supermarket to find out this information – you can also find the information on the internet!

4 Provide arguments for a debate that says that 'local shops provide the best value for money'. (Remember that you should consider arguments both for and against the motion.)

3 Shopping on the internet

What's all this about?

Home shopping offers both convenience and choice and is no more difficult than making a telephone call or clicking a mouse. No queues or crowds, no traffic and no need to worry about the weather.

However, buying from a catalogue or window shopping on the internet poses its own problems and it is best to be wary when shopping from home. If you shop for goods or services by telephone, mail order, fax, digital television, or on the internet, you now have new consumer rights to clear information, a cooling-off period and protection against credit card fraud.

Clear information
Information must include a description of the goods or services, the price (including all taxes), arrangements for payment and arrangements for delivery.

A cooling-off period
The seller must provide written information on when and how you can cancel your order or your contract.

Protection against credit card fraud
Regulations make it safer for you to use your credit card or payment card on the internet, over the phone or for other types of home shopping.

What does it mean?

Shopping on the internet

Increasingly, the internet is being used to buy and sell goods and most things from cars to cheese can now be bought over the internet. When using the internet to buy goods, it is important to make sure that the site you are using is safe and secure.

You will usually be asked to fill in a form like this one.

TOMPA'S QUICKI MART
Shopping on the net

◀ **BACK**

Email Address*		Please ensure that you type this accurately as you will need it to log into the site in future. (We will also confirm any orders to this address.)
Password*		(Minimum 6 characters)
Confirm Password*		
Title*		
First Name*		
Initial(s)*		
Surname*		
Address Line 1*		
Address Line 2*		
Address Line 3		
Address Line 4		
Country*		
Postcode*		
Telephone (day)*		(We will call you only if there is a query regarding an order you have placed.)
Telephone (evening)*		
Gender*		
Date of Birth		(dd/mm/yyyy)

(Mandatory fields are marked*)

The company will then provide you with a username (usually your name) and a password which you will be able to use in all future transactions.

Using your cards

When you buy something over the internet, you'll need to pay using a credit or debit card. You may have to ask an adult to do this for you, using their card if you do not have one.

Most web retailers offer you the option of sending your credit card details via a secure (encrypted) page. Your browser will tell you whether the page you are on is secure. You can usually see a padlock symbol at the bottom of your screen.

If you can't see the secure symbol, then the site is probably not secure...don't use it!

If someone makes dishonest or fraudulent use of your card then you can cancel the payment and the card issuer must refund the money to your account. Of course, the card issuer will want you to tell them as soon as possible if your card has been lost or stolen, or if you find out that someone is using your card details dishonestly.

You also have some extra protection if you make payment using a credit card. If you have a claim against the seller (for example, if the goods were never supplied, if they were not as described or if they were faulty) then you may also have a claim against your credit card issuer, even if you only used the card to pay a deposit.

Shopping abroad

While the internet makes it easy for you to shop abroad, you might want to consider the following.

- Will it work? Standards and systems vary between countries and you need to make certain that electrical equipment from abroad will work in the UK.

- Is it a good deal? When deciding, take into account the cost of converting currency or arranging for money to be sent abroad.

- Are there hidden costs? Check for hidden costs such as VAT, customs duties, delivery charges, postage and packaging.

- Does it have a guarantee? Check that the guarantee is valid in the UK, or whether you will have to return the product to the supplier's country if there is a problem.

- How easy will it be to sort out any problems? Always consider what will happen if problems arise, especially if you will have to take legal action abroad.

Item	£20.00
VAT	£3.50
Customs	£4.00
Post and Packing	£18.75
	£46.25

What do you know?

1 One of the advantages of shopping on the internet is that it is quick and convenient. One of the disadvantages is that you need a computer (or an interactive television) to connect to the internet. Write down three other advantages and disadvantages of shopping on the internet.

advantages	disadvantages
Quick	You need a computer

2 Carry out an internet survey to find a site to buy each of the following. In each case, write down the website address and the name of the company.

   Airline tickets, books, cars, clothes, compact discs, computers, concert tickets, food, holidays, houses, insurance, theatre tickets, train tickets…

	web address
Airline tickets	www…
Books	

3 Carry out an internet survey to compare the prices of a typical shopping basket on the internet and at your local supermarket. (You could use your shopping basket from page 8 question 3.) Which is the best value and why? (Remember that you might need to take service charges and transport costs into account.)

4 Provide arguments for a debate on 'Does the internet provide the best value for money?' Remember that you should consider arguments both for and against the motion.

5 Carry out your own statistical survey on the use of the internet for shopping.
   You may wish to consider the following questions.

   ● Who uses the internet most for shopping (by age, by gender etc.)?
   ● How often do these people use the internet for shopping?
   ● What sort of things do people most often buy on the internet?
   ● How happy are people with their experience of internet shopping?

4 Income – Part I

What's all this about?

Millionaires, billionaires, trillionaires, …

The American multi-millionaire Paul Getty once said 'If you can count your money then you are not really a rich man'.

Did you know that Bill Gates is the richest man in the world? He is said to be worth £54 billion (a bit more by the time you have read this).

Can you imagine £54 billion? That is £54 000 000 000.

How long would it take you to save that amount in pocket money or earn it in a part time job?

In this section we will look at different ways in which work is paid for.

What calculations do you need to do to work out your income?

Look at these job adverts:

PAPER ROUND

Payment:
£3.90 per day + 3p per newspaper delivered

CLEANING JOB

Payment:
£4.50 per hour (weekend work at time and a half)

These two jobs are advertised in a local newsagent's window – but which one is the better paid?

Work it out

In order to work out which is better paid, you are going to have to do a little bit of work.

PAPER ROUND

Payment:
£3.90 per day + 3p per newspaper delivered

◀ · · · · · · · · · ·

For the paper round, the answer will depend on:

How many days?

How many papers?

5 days and 20 newspapers

$$\begin{aligned}
\text{1 day's pay} &= £3.90 + (20 \times 3\text{p}) \\
&= £3.90 + 60\text{p} \\
&= £4.50 \\
\text{So 5 days' pay} &= 5 \times £4.50 \\
&= £22.50
\end{aligned}$$

or 7 days and 16 newspapers

$$\begin{aligned}
\text{1 day's pay} &= £3.90 + (16 \times 3\text{p}) \\
&= £3.90 + 48\text{p} \\
&= £4.38 \\
\text{So 7 days' pay} &= 7 \times £4.38 \\
&= £30.66
\end{aligned}$$

CLEANING JOB

Payment:
£4.50 per hour (weekend work at time and a half)

◀ · · · · · · · · · ·

For the cleaning job, the answer will depend on:

How many hours?

How much at weekends?

$$\begin{aligned}
\text{5 hours' pay} &= 5 \times £4.50 \\
&= £22.50
\end{aligned}$$

but 5 hours' pay at the weekend…

$$\begin{aligned}
\text{weekend hourly rate} &= 1\tfrac{1}{2} \times £4.50 \\
&= £6.75
\end{aligned}$$

$$\begin{aligned}
\text{so 5 hours' pay} &= 5 \times £6.75 \\
&= £33.75
\end{aligned}$$

So which is the better-paid job?
Why?

What does it mean?

There are a number of different ways in which work is paid for:

Wages

A wage can be paid daily, weekly or monthly. There is now a legal minimum wage of £3.70 per hour, which an employer must pay to his or her employees.

A wage of 35 hours at £4.20 will pay

$$35 \times £4.20 = £147 \text{ per week}$$

35 hours at £4.20 per hour

Salaries

"£12 000 per annum"

A salary is the same as a wage but is expressed in terms of a year's pay.
£12 000 per annum means £12 000 each year (or £1000 each month)

Overtime

Overtime is money paid for working more than the agreed number of hours each week. Overtime is often paid at a different rate such as 'time and a half', which means one and a half times the normal rate or 'double time', which means two times the normal rate.

OFFICE WORK

Payment:
£4.80 per hour (evening work at time and a half, weekend work at double time)

Payment for this office work is:

Evening work at $1\frac{1}{2} \times £4.80 = £7.20$ per hour

Weekend rate at $2 \times £4.80 = £9.60$ per hour

What do you know?

1 Andy is paid £4.50 per hour for a 40 hour week. Overtime is paid at double time.
How much will he be paid for a full week plus two hours overtime?

2 Ceri is paid £6.70 per hour for a 38 hour week. Overtime is paid at time and a half.
How much will she be paid for a full week plus four hours overtime?

3 ● What sort of jobs do you and your friends have?
   ● Which jobs are well paid and which jobs are badly paid?
   ● Why?

4 Have you ever thought about how much different people earn?
Find examples of different jobs from adverts in local and national papers.
   ● Which jobs are well paid and which jobs are badly paid?
   ● Why are some jobs better paid than others?
   ● Which jobs do you think should be better paid?

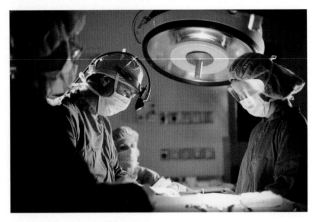

5 Write down three advantages and three disadvantages of having a minimum wage.

6 Which job pays the most money?

JOB A

Payment:

1p on the first day,
2p on the second day,
4p on the third day,
8p on the fourth day,
...for thirty days

JOB B

Payment:

A lump sum of
£20 000,
to be paid at the
end of thirty days.

Try this question out and you'll realise that things aren't always what they seem...

5 Income – Part II

What's all this about?

Imagine that you were given a job that paid you £1.00 a second.

What a great job that would be!

How long would it take you to earn £1000?
How long would it take you to earn £1 million?
How long would it take you to earn £1 billion?

Remember that you cannot possibly work 24 hours a day.

In this section we will look at some other ways in which work is paid for.

What calculations do you need to do to work out your income?
What is the difference between income and take home pay?

'For I don't care too much for money. For money can't buy me love.'

John Lennon

Look at the following:

FLOWER SELLER

Payment:
You will be paid 8% of
the money recieved

SEALING ENVELOPES

Payment:
£2.90 + 1p for each
envelope sealed

These are two jobs advertised in a local newsagent's window, but which one is the better paid?

Work it out

Commission

Commission is payment for work based on the number of sales… so the more you sell, the more you receive in commission.

> ## FLOWER SELLER
>
> Payment:
> You will be paid 8% of
> the money recieved

◄••••••••••••••••

> Here, the amount of pay depends on the amount of money received.
>
> You need to calculate 8% of the money received.

How to find a percentage

You can skip this bit if you are confident with percentages…

Step 1: Find 1% by dividing by 100.

Step 2: Multiply to find the required percentage.

> So percentages are really quite easy

For example… to find 10% of £400

$$1\% \text{ of } £400 = £400 \div 100 = £4$$
$$10\% \text{ of } £400 = 10 \times £4 = £40$$

Similarly … to find 22% of £15

$$1\% \text{ of } £15 = £15 \div 100 = £0.15$$
$$22\% \text{ of } £15 = 22 \times £0.15 = £3.30$$

Calculations for the flower seller:

If the amount of money received = £10

$$1\% \text{ of } £10 = £10 \div 100 = £0.10$$
$$8\% \text{ of } £10 = 8 \times £0.10 = £0.80$$
$$\text{Payment} = £0.80$$

or

If the amount of money received = £55

$$1\% \text{ of } £55 = £55 \div 100 = £0.55$$
$$8\% \text{ of } £55 = 8 \times £0.55 = £4.40$$
$$\text{Payment} = £4.40$$

How much is a bunch of flowers?
How many bunches of flowers can you sell in an hour?
So what is your rate of pay (per hour)?

Piecework

Piecework is a payment for each piece of work done. It persuades people to work harder and is often combined with wages or salaries.

SEALING ENVELOPES

Payment:
£2.90 + 1p for each
envelope sealed

◄ • • • • • • • • • • •

Here, the amount of pay depends on the number of envelopes sealed.

You need to know the number of envelopes sealed.

Calculations for sealing envelopes:

5 envelopes pay	£2.90 + (5 × 1p)	= £2.95
1000 envelopes pay	£2.90 + (1000 × 1p)	= £12.90

How long does it take you to seal an envelope?
How long would it take to seal 1000 envelopes?
So what is your rate of pay (per hour)?

Which is the better paid job?   Why?

What does it mean?

Easy come, easy go...

Of course, the amount you earn is not the same as the amount of money you actually receive – a typical wage slip will include earnings and deductions.

Income tax
This is money paid to the government from your earnings.
You can find out more about taxes in Chapters 6 and 7.

COMPANY NAME: **ANY COMPANY LTD**			
Department: – STAFF			
Pay and Allowances	**Deductions (R = Refund)**	**Balance and totals to date**	
Basic Pay 1791.66	INCOME TAX 277.09	INCOME TAX 1962.35	
	NAT INS 117.26	NAT INS 820.82	
	PENSION 50.00	PENSION 250.00	
TOTAL 1791.66	TOTAL 444.35	Net Pay 1347.31	

	DATE	DEPT.	PAY POINT	TAX CODE	EMPLOYEE NO.	EMPLOYEE NAME	NET PAY
1	06/09/01	1		453L	1	Mr. N. E. BODY	

National Insurance contributions
This is money that the government collects to pay for state pensions and some other state benefits, including benefits paid to people who are too ill to work.

Pension contributions
These are deductions from your wages to provide you with extra income when you retire. Unlike income tax and National Insurance contributions, pension contributions are not compulsory, but most people decide to contribute because the pensions paid by the state are very low.

What do you know?

1 If you needed to earn £1000 as quickly as possible, which of these jobs would you take?

PAPER ROUND

Payment:
£3.90 per day + 3p per
newspaper delivered

CLEANING JOB

Payment:
£4.50 per hour (weekend
work at time and a half)

FLOWER SELLER

Payment:
You will be paid 8% of
the money recieved

SEALING ENVELOPES

Payment:
£2.90 + 1p for each
envelope sealed

Give reasons for your choice.
Don't forget to explain the assumptions you
have made.

2 A travel agent receives a basic wage of £280 a week
plus 1% commission on all holidays sold. One week
the travel agent sells £6800 worth of holidays.

- How much commission does the travel agent earn
  in this week?
- How much does the travel agent earn altogether in
  this week?

3 Sarah earns £3.20 per day plus 8p for every
parcel that she addresses.
How much does she earn on each of
the following days?

Friday	80 parcels
Saturday	75 parcels
Sunday	36 parcels

4 Write down a list of jobs that are likely
to pay:

- commission
- piecework.

5 Design a wage slip that can be generated by a computer.
Think carefully about what information will be included.

*You might use a
spreadsheet to work out
deductions and calculate
the final total.*

6 Taxing problems

What's all this about?

Benjamin Franklin, the famous American statesman, scientist and writer, once said:

'In this world nothing is certain but death and taxes.'

Nowadays most taxes (for example income tax and Value Added Tax) are collected by central government, although local authorities also collect money to help pay for services such as street lights and rubbish collection. This is known as council tax.

Taxes can be divided into the following two groups.

Direct tax
A direct tax is a tax on an individual's money, for example income tax on earnings or inheritance tax on gifts. The Inland Revenue usually collects direct taxes.

Indirect tax
An indirect tax is a tax on goods or services that you buy, for example Value Added Tax or VAT. Customs and Excise usually collect indirect taxes.

Inland Revenue

The Inland Revenue is a government department that has responsibility for assessing and collecting direct taxes and National Insurance contributions. The Inland Revenue collects nearly two-fifths of the government's income each year.

Income tax

Income tax is a tax on income that includes earnings from work, expenses payments, benefits (such as company cars), interest on savings, dividends from shares as well as tips and bonuses.

Would you believe it?

It costs the government over 1p to collect every £100 of income tax. Ten years ago, it cost the government $2\frac{1}{2}$p to collect every £100 of income tax!

Did you know?

William Pitt the Younger introduced income tax in 1799 in order to fund the Napoleonic Wars. Income tax as we know it began in 1842, when wealthy people paid the equivalent of 3p for every pound of their income. In 1941 the standard rate of income tax reached its highest level when it was increased to the equivalent of 50p in the pound.

What does it mean?

Tax allowance
Everyone, even children, is given a personal allowance. This is the amount of income that you can have before you start having to pay tax.

Taxable income
Taxable income is the amount of income on which income tax is to be paid. The amount of taxable income is usually found by subtracting allowances from income.

    taxable income = annual income − personal allowances

Tax bands
Your taxable income is divided into slices called 'bands'. Tax on the first slice is charged at a fairly low rate. The next slice is charged at a higher rate and the top slice is charged at the highest rate of all.

Work it out

Victoria's sister earns £420.00 per month in her part time job. She has a tax allowance of £4385 a year and pays 10% on the first £1520 of her taxable income.

Do I really have to pay all this tax?

Victoria wants to check how much tax her sister should pay.

    annual income = £420 × 12 = £5040

    taxable income = annual income − personal allowance
                   = £5040 − £4385
                   = £655

Tax rates

Starting rate	10% on first £1520 of taxable income
Basic rate	22% on taxable income over £1520 up to £28 400
Higher rate	40% on taxable income over £28 400

The tax rates given are for 2000–2001. You might want to find out what the latest tax rates are.

Tax at lower rate = 10% of £655

               = £65.50

$$1\% \text{ of } £655 = £655 \div 100 = £6.55$$
$$10\% \text{ of } £655 = 10 \times £6.55 = £65.50$$

Stevie has an income of £1000 per month. He has a single person's tax allowance of £4385. How much tax does Stevie pay each year? (Use the tax rates in the table.)

Annual income   = £1000 × 12 = £12 000

Personal allowances = £4385

Taxable income   = Annual income − personal allowances

                   = £12 000 − £4385

                   = £7615

Stevie pays 10% tax (lower rate) on the first £1520 of taxable income and 22% tax (basic rate) on income above £1520 up to £28 400.

On £7615, Stevie pays 10% tax on the first £1520 and 22% tax on the remaining £6095 because

Tax at lower rate = 10% of £1520

               = £152

$$1\% \text{ of } £1520 = £1520 \div 100 = £15.20$$
$$10\% \text{ of } £1520 = 10 \times £15.20 = £152$$

Tax at basic rate = 22% of £6095

               = £1340.90

$$1\% \text{ of } £6095 = £6095 \div 100 = £60.95$$
$$22\% \text{ of } £6095 = 22 \times £60.95 = £1340.90$$

Total tax   = £152 + £1340.90

               = £1492.90

tax at lower rate
+ tax at basic rate

Stevie pays £1492.90 tax altogether each year.

What do you know?

1 Jacqui earns £130 per week. She has a personal allowance of £4385. What is her taxable income?

2 Jeremy has a part time job and earns £66 per week. His personal allowance is £4385. What is his taxable income?

3 Rupesh earns £5200 one year. He has a tax allowance of £4195 and pays 10p in the pound on his taxable income. Calculate how much tax Rupesh pays per year.

4 The following table shows how £100 of tax is spent by the government:

Social Security	£30
Defence	£7
Debt charges	£9
Public order & safety	£5
Education	£11
Health	£17
Other	£21

Display the information as a bar chart or a pie chart.

5 If you were in charge of government spending how would you spend each £100 of tax? Don't forget to give reasons for your answers.

6 How much is the council tax for the area where you live?
Why do different areas pay different council taxes?
What sort of things does your council tax pay for?

7 How good a detective are you?
Find out why the tax year runs from the 6th April to the 5th April the following year. What has this got to do with the Gregorian calendar, some missing days in September 1752 and the re-imposition of income tax in 1842?

7 More taxing problems – VAT

What's all this about?

We have already mentioned that indirect taxes are taxes on goods or services and that they are usually collected by Customs and Excise.

Customs & Excise

Customs and Excise is one of the oldest government departments. In England, the first customs duty was collected in 743 from medieval ships and, in 1203, a duty of one-fifteenth was placed on all imports and exports. In 1643, beer and spirits duty was introduced as a temporary measure, to provide funds for the Civil War.

Customs and Excise brings in around 40 per cent of the government's income each year, as well as being responsible for protecting society against the growing threat of drugs, firearms and pornographic material. In the last year for which information was available, the department had seized more than £3.3 billion worth of drugs, 200 illegal imports of firearms and almost 3000 endangered live animals and birds.

Value Added Tax (VAT)

Value Added Tax (VAT) was introduced into the United Kingdom on 1 April 1973. It replaced Purchase Tax and Selective Employment Tax. The government collects VAT by requiring businesses to add VAT to the prices of their goods and services. The original VAT rate was 10%, so was quite easy to work out! Nowadays, the standard rate of VAT is 17.5%.

There are three VAT rates in the UK:

- Standard rate of 17.5% charged on most goods and services.
- Reduced rate of 5% charged on domestic fuel.
- Zero-rated (0%) – some things such as rail fares and books are not taxed.

Would you believe it?

A business selling live maggots to anglers from vending machines on garage forecourts claimed it should not have to add VAT to its prices because the maggots were fish food (VAT free). The courts disagreed saying VAT must be charged because the maggots were not food, but bait to lure the fish.

25

Working it out

Joel has decided to use his birthday money to buy a mountain bike. He sees two bikes advertised in his local paper.

Sometimes we say £400 plus VAT instead of £400 excluding VAT.

Which of the advertised mountain bikes is the best buy?

To find which is the best buy, Joel needs to calculate the cost of the second bike by adding on VAT at a rate of 17.5%.

So the VAT on the second bike is 17.5% of £400.

$$1\% \text{ of } £400 = £400 \div 100 = £4$$
$$17.5\% \text{ of } £400 = 17.5 \times £4 = £70$$

So the VAT on the second bike is £70.

Now this VAT needs to be added to the original cost.

So the total cost of the second bike is £400 + £70 = £470.

We can now see that the bike from BIKES R US is cheaper.

What does it mean?

A useful way to find out the VAT is to find 10%, then 5%, then 2.5%.

For example, the VAT on the second bike is 17.5% of £400.

$$
\begin{aligned}
10\% \text{ of } £400 &= £40 \\
5\% \text{ of } £400 &= £20 \\
\underline{2.5\% \text{ of } £400} &= \underline{£10} \\
\text{adding } 17.5\% \text{ of } £400 &= £70
\end{aligned}
$$

So the VAT on the second mountain bike is £70 (as before).

If you increase an amount by 17.5% then decrease the same amount by 17.5%, you don't get back to where you started.

For example, after the bike is increased by 17.5% the cost is £470.

You're a good friend so I'll give you a discount of 17.5%

If you are offered a 17.5% discount on the bike, how much will you pay?

First we need to find 17.5% of £470.

$$
\begin{aligned}
10\% \text{ of } £470 &= £47 \\
5\% \text{ of } £470 &= £23.50 \\
\underline{2.5\% \text{ of } £470} &= \underline{£11.75} \\
\text{adding } 17.5\% \text{ of } £470 &= £82.25
\end{aligned}
$$

Now this decrease needs to be taken away from the cost.

$$
\begin{aligned}
\text{Discounted cost} &= £470 - £82.25 \\
&= £387.75 \dots \text{ not } £400!
\end{aligned}
$$

Try this out on some different amounts.

Does it always happen?

Here's an easy way to calculate VAT ... in your head!

What do you know?

1 Find the total purchase price for the following items:

    a) a DVD player priced at £600 + VAT

    b) a TV and video priced at £450 + VAT

    c) a digital camera priced at £225 + VAT.

2 An invoice is received for £92.00 before VAT at 17.5%.
What is the total cost of the bill with VAT?

3 A computer is priced at £2350, which includes VAT at $17\frac{1}{2}$%.
What is the cost of the computer without the VAT?

> The answer is not
> £1938.75!

4 Make a list of items that include VAT.
Make a list of items that do not include VAT (i.e. they are zero rated or exempt).

5 What are the VAT rates in other European countries?
Display the information as a bar chart.

6 Geoffrey Chaucer and Robert Burns were both connected with Customs and Excise. Carry out your own research to find out about these two people and their links with Customs and Excise.

Geoffrey Chaucer

Robert Burns

8 Who pays the phone bill?

What's all this about?

The two basic types of mobile phone tariff are conventional tariffs and pre-pay tariffs.

Conventional tariffs

With this type of tariff, you sign a contract to use the phone for a minimum period, usually a year. There is a penalty if you give up the phone early. You have to be at least 18 years old, although you could try to persuade an adult to sign the contract for you.

Pre-pay tariffs

With this type of tariff, you do not sign a contract and there is no penalty if you give up the phone early. You pay your bill by buying cards that credit money on to your phone. As you make calls, the money credited to your phone is used up.

Things to watch out for with mobile bills

- Calls cost more if you make them in peak times. The definition of peak times varies so check the small print very carefully.
- Usually, you pay extra if you phone another mobile phone – especially if it's on another provider's network.
- International calls cost extra and you might need to speak to your provider to allow international calls to be made.
- Lots of phones let you send text messages to other people who also have text phones – sending text messages is generally cheaper than making a call.

Harish wants to buy a mobile phone and is comparing the costs for different mobile phone tariffs.

> **Would you believe it?**
>
> There are over 140 different ways of paying for mobile phones (called tariffs). Which one suits you best will depend on when and how often you use your phone.

TARIFF A	TARIFF B
Cost just 5p per minute any time and any day	*£10 per month and only 1p per minute*

Which of these tariffs is the best for Harish?

Work it out

To decide which of the tariffs is the best buy for Harish, you need to know how many minutes Harish spends on the phone.

If Harish does not use his phone at all for one month…

> Harish would need to pay the £10 regardless of how many calls he makes

TARIFF A
Cost = £0.00
✓ cheaper

TARIFF B
Cost = £10.00

If Harish uses 100 minutes of calls in one month…

TARIFF A
Cost = 100 x 5p
= £5.00
✓ cheaper

TARIFF B
Cost = £10.00
+ 100 x 1p
= £11.00

If Harish uses 200 minutes of calls in one month…

TARIFF A
Cost = 200 x 5p
= £10.00
✓ cheaper

TARIFF B
Cost = £10.00
+ 200 x 1p
= £12.00

If Harish uses 300 minutes of calls in one month…

TARIFF A
Cost = 300 x 5p
= £15.00

TARIFF B
Cost = £10.00
+ 300 x 1p
= £13.00
✓ cheaper

Can you work out how many minutes Harish can use before Tariff B is his cheaper option?

One possible way to see which tariff is best is to draw a table or graph of the information.

Number of minutes in one month	Cost for tariff A	Cost for tariff B
0	£0.00	£10.00
100	£5.00	£11.00
200	£10.00	£12.00
300	£15.00	£13.00
400	£20.00	£14.00

You can see that tariff A is cheaper up to 200 minutes and tariff B is cheaper from 300 minutes upwards so Harish has to use between 200 and 300 minutes before tariff B becomes cheaper.

To find the values you could keep trying different values or else draw a graph.

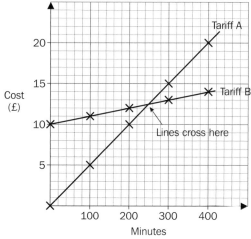

If you are very good at algebra then you can also solve these using simultaneous equations ... but maybe graphs are easier?

From the table you can see that the lines cross at 250 minutes.

For 250 minutes in one month...

The graph tells you that:
- below 250 minutes tariff A is cheaper
- at 250 minutes both tariffs cost the same
- above 250 minutes tariff B is cheaper.

So mathematics can be very useful in helping us decide which is the best value for money.

What do you know?

1 Which of the tariffs is the best buy? (Remember that you will have to consider how many minutes are spent on the phone.)

ANYTIME TARIFF Costs just 3p per minute any time and any day	**PENNY TARIFF** £6 per month and only 1p per minute
TARIFF FIVE Costs just 5p per minute any time and any day	**TENNER TARIFF** £10 per month and only 1p per minute

2 Find out the tariffs for three different mobile phones and make a comparison to find the best value.
Don't forget to include a note of any assumptions that you make.

3 Do you think that mobile phones are a good thing?
Write down three advantages and disadvantages of mobile phones.

4 Carry out a survey on the use of the mobile phones.
You may wish to consider the following questions.

- Who uses mobile phones the most (by age, by gender, etc.)?
- How long is spent on mobile phones (on weekdays, weekends, evenings)?
- What are mobile phones used for (work, recreation, text messaging, internet)?
- How happy are people with their mobile phones?

9 Banking on it

What's all this about?

Have you ever wanted to be a millionaire? What would you do with that much money? Where would you keep it?

How much space would £1 million in £1 coins take up? Or £1 million in £5 notes? Or £1 million in £50 notes?

Nowadays, we do not have to bury our money or hide it under the mattress to keep it safe, but have you ever thought where you would keep your money if there were no banks, building societies or credit unions?

Banks

Banks are companies whose business is handling people's money. They provide a variety of services to depositors (e.g. bank accounts) and borrowers (e.g. loans). Banks are owned by shareholders so that any profits made are given back to the shareholders.

Building societies

Building societies offer similar services to banks, but they are owned by the customers so that any profits made belong to them.

Credit unions

Credit unions are very popular in the USA, Canada and Ireland. They are organisations that provide savings facilities for depositors and loans for borrowers. The members must share some common bond, such as working for the same employer, living in the same area, or belonging to the same church.

Bob Hope, the famous American comedian, once said, 'A bank is a place that will lend you money if you can prove you don't need it'.

Would you believe it?

A long time ago, most people used to hide their money by burying it underground.

Would you believe it?

The Bank of England produces 1 400 000 000 notes each year. Laid end to end they would stretch half way to the moon!

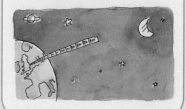

Work it out

Statements

When you have a bank or building society account you will receive regular statements.

Cheques (CHQ)
If you have paid someone by writing them a cheque, the cheque number will be shown ('100311' in this example) and the amount paid out of your account to the person ('£17.00' in this case).

Overdrawn (D)
If the debits from your account are more than your balance then your account will be overdrawn and you will have a negative balance. Here, the letter 'D' after the balance shows this.

Sort Code
This is a six-figure number that identifies your particular branch.

Account number
This is a number that identifies your individual account with the bank.

Balance brought forward
This is the amount of money that you had in your account at the end of the last statement period.

Direct debit (DD)
A direct debit is an authority given to your bank to allow a company to take the money direct from your account to pay bills or repay loans.

SAFEHANDS BANK PLC
15 Moneybags Lane, Sheckleton GR20 5AB

MR U R RICH
Account number: 00220001
Sheet 46   Sort Code 50-33-01

			PAID OUT	PAID IN	BALANCE
18 Jul 02		Balance brought forward			£ 40.00
19 Jul 02	CHQ	100311	17.00		£ 23.00
28 Jul 02	DD	SOUTHERN ELECTRIC	32.00		£ 9.00 D
31 Jul 02	CR	WEPAE		£1,000	£ 991.00
01 Aug 02	SO	NEEDY I B	15.00		£ 976.00
10 Aug 02	CR	PAID IN AT SAFEHANDS BK		50.00	£ 1,026.00
11 Aug 02	ATM	Cash	10.00		£ 1,016.00
14 Aug 02	CR	Net interest		0.18	£ 1,016.18
14 Aug 02		Balance carried forward			£ 1,016.18

Credit (CR)
A credit is any amount paid into your account by whatever means. There are three credits listed here.

Cash machine (ATM)
This shows the amount that you have taken out of your account using your cash card in a cash machine (Automated Teller Machine).

Standing orders (SO)
A standing order is an instruction to your bank to make regular payments of a fixed amount to someone else or to another account in your own name (for example a regular savings account).

Balance carried forward
This is the amount of money that you have left in your account at the end of the statement period.

Debit (DR)
A debit is any money paid out of your account by whatever means. Cheques, payments by debit cards, direct debits and standing orders are all examples of debits.

Interest

Interest is usually expressed as so much per cent a year – for example, an interest rate of 6% tells you that for every £100 you invest for one year, you can expect £6 in interest.

However, interest which is paid more regularly is better than interest which you receive only once a year. This is because you get interest on your interest which can boost the overall total.

What happens if you deposit £100 and the interest rate is 6% a year?

If the interest is applied at the end of the year:

> At the end of the year
> Interest = 6% of £100 = £6
> Total amount at the end of the year = £100 + £6 = £106

If the interest is applied at six-monthly intervals:

> At the end of six months
> Interest = $\frac{1}{2} \times$ 6% of £100 = £3
> (remember that it is only for $\frac{1}{2}$ of the year)
> Total amount at the end of six months = £100 + £3 = £103

At the end of the year

> Interest = $\frac{1}{2} \times$ 6% of £103 = £3.09
> Total amount at the end of the year = £103 + £3.09
> = £106.09

Very interesting!

Annual Equivalent Rate (AER)

A useful way to compare interest rates is to use the **Annual Equivalent Rate (AER)**, which compares the interest payable on bank and building society accounts.

The AER taken illustrates the rate you could pay if your interest rate was paid and compounded on an annual basis, excluding any bonuses.

You do not need to know how to work out the AER. All you need to know is that an account with a high AER gives a better return for your money than one with a low AER.

What do you know?

1 Copy and complete the bank statement to show the following transactions:

A cheque payment to Marks and Spencer of £36, cheque number 100312, on the 20th August.
A cash machine withdrawal of £30 on the 16th August.
A direct debit to Abbey National of £120 on the 25th August.
A credit of 24p net interest on the 22nd August.

SAFEHANDS BANK PLC
15 Moneybags Lane, Sheckleton GR20 5AB

MR U R RICH
Account number: 00220001
Sheet 47   Sort Code 50-33-01

		PAID OUT	PAID IN	BALANCE
14 Aug 02	Balance brought forward			£ 1,016.00

2 In the earlier example, you saw that if you deposit £100 and the interest rate is 6% per year then:

If the interest is applied at the end of the year,
the total amount = £106
If the interest is applied at six-monthly intervals,
the total amount = £106.09

What would be the total amount

a) if the interest were applied quarterly?
b) if the interest were applied monthly?

How much more do you think the interest would be if you applied it daily or hourly?

3 Carry out your own research on the differences between a current account and a savings account.

4 Write down three advantages and disadvantages of

- postal banking
- telephone banking
- internet banking.

10 ATM – all that money

What's all this about?

The first cash machines, or Automated Teller Machines (ATMs), were introduced to the UK in 1967 by Barclays Bank. These early machines had limited functions and dispensed fixed amounts of cash in exchange for tokens. In the early 1970s, magnetic strip technology enabled cash machines to dispense cash.

Today, cash machines are available 24 hours a day, 365 days a year. They provide customers with a wide range of services so that, at most ATMs, you can:

- withdraw money
- check your balance
- get a printout of your balance
- transfer money
- change your PIN number
- order a cheque book
- order a statement.

Would you believe it?

There are over 28 000 cash machines in Great Britain and over 112 million cards that can be used in them. That is over 4000 cards for each cash machine!

Nearly two-thirds of all adults are regular users of ATMs, with around 5 million withdrawals each day at an average of £55 each. That is a total of £275 000 000 every single day!

There were approximately 2 billion withdrawals made from cash machines last year. Can you imagine being stuck at the end of that queue to get your money?

Younger people use cash machines more than the elderly do. Younger customers also withdraw cash more frequently than older customers do.

What does it mean?

Transaction slip

The most common use for ATMs is to withdraw money. It is always a good idea to obtain a receipt for any transactions.

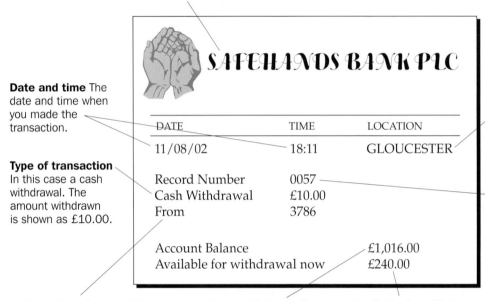

Name of organisation which owns or runs the cash machine This information tells you the ATM belongs to Safehands Bank PLC.

Date and time The date and time when you made the transaction.

Type of transaction In this case a cash withdrawal. The amount withdrawn is shown as £10.00.

Location The town or, in larger places, the road or building, in which the ATM is situated.

Record number A number that identifies the particular withdrawal. This helps the bank or building society trace the transaction in the case of a dispute.

From An indication of the account from which you have withdrawn the money. In most cases it will include the last few digits of your account number (for security reasons the whole code is not given).

Account balance Some (but not all) ATMs check the balance remaining in your account after the withdrawal and give it on the print-out.

Available for withdrawal now Some (but not all) ATMs show the maximum you can withdraw if you use your card again immediately. Usually, there is a limit, such as £250 a day.

Using ATMs

Most banks and building societies have arrangements so that you can use any cash machine to withdraw cash. Since January 2001, institutions have agreed not to charge other banks' or building societies' customers for using their ATMs.

However, there are a number of non-bank or building society ATMs (usually situated in pubs, corner shops, hospitals and petrol stations) which do charge a fee. This should be advertised on the screen before the money is withdrawn.

Personal Identification Number or PIN

In order to withdraw money from an ATM a customer needs a card issued by the appropriate bank or building society and the correct Personal Identification Number (PIN).

The PIN is a four-digit number, which you can consider to be your very own password. It is important that you do not tell anyone else your PIN and that you do not write it down.

It makes sense to choose a number you can easily memorise, but avoid obvious numbers like 1234, or numbers related to your date of birth (which may be on other documents kept in a wallet, say, with a lost or stolen cash card).

ATM fraud

Last year, nearly £200 million was stolen through plastic card fraud. However, cash card fraud accounted for only a small part (around 6%) of the losses. Frauds include stealing cards and PIN numbers and making fake cards.

Remember that if your card is fraudulently used then the maximum loss you personally face is £50. However, you might have to bear the whole loss if, for example, you have told someone your PIN or lent someone your card.

Would you believe it?

A talking ATM that greets customers and asks them how much money they want to withdraw recently went on show in London following a successful public trial in Canada. The new machine, known as Stella, does not use a keyboard. Instead, it will identify the customer by reading their iris (the coloured part of the eye) with high definition cameras to provide virtually foolproof identification.

What do you know?

1 Write down three advantages and three disadvantages of using an ATM as opposed to using a bank counter.

2 Produce a map of your local area and show the positions of any ATMs on your map. What do you notice?

3 Design your own poster to stop plastic card fraud. You might want to include the following advice:
- Never throw away transaction slips which include your card number on them.
- Always check your statements against the transaction slips.
- Never give out your card details (including the PIN number) to other people.

4 Carry out a survey about how people use ATMs. You may wish to include the following questions:
- What do people use ATMs for?
- How long do people spend using ATMs?
- What time of day is the busiest for using ATMs?

5 Write an essay describing your vision of what ATMs will be like in 50 years time.

11 Who needs cash?

What's all this about?

Until the end of the 19th century, only wealthy people had access to credit so most people had to pay for things with cash. If they needed to borrow money then they had to turn to moneylenders or pawnbrokers. This was often an unreliable and expensive form of credit, so it was not very popular.

During the 19th and early 20th centuries, as people became richer and had more money to spend on consumables and other items, credit arrangements with shops became more widely available. A number of finance companies were created in the later part of the 19th century to meet this demand.

The earliest charge cards were used in America in the 1920s and were issued by oil companies and hotels to trustworthy customers. The first modern card was issued by the Diners Club in 1950. The company charged its customers an annual fee and invoiced them on a monthly or annual basis.

The next major charge card was provided by American Express in 1958. American Express introduced its card to Britain in 1963. The first British credit card was the Barclaycard (based on BankAmericard, now part of Visa) which was introduced by Barclays Bank in 1966. The rival Access card which was linked to MasterCard did not appear until 1972.

Today, there are nearly 120 million bank and building society plastic cards in issue in the UK and over 85% of the adult population hold one or more plastic cards. Approximately 3.8 billion purchases were made with plastic cards last year, this is expected to increase almost two-fold in the next ten years.

> **Would you believe it?**
>
> A £5 note costs less than three pence to produce so it isn't worth that much really!

> **Would you believe it?**
>
> In 2000, there was an average of 169 cards for every 100 people in the UK, and 60 cards for every 100 people in Italy.

What does it mean?

Today, there are more than 500 000 places in the UK where you can use credit and debit cards. These include shops, garages, travel agents, hotels and many other outlets. Credit and debit cards can also be used to pay for goods or services ordered over the telephone, through the mail and over the Internet.

Different types of cards

Cheque guarantee card

Cheque guarantee cards are cards that guarantee a cheque up to a particular value (usually £50 or £100). By writing your cheque guarantee card number on the back of the cheque, the retailer will be paid by your bank. A cheque guarantee card will usually only be available if you are over 18 and have a regular income.

Cash withdrawal card

Cash cards are cards issued by banks and building societies to allow the owner to withdraw money or check his or her balance at an ATM. You will usually have to be 11 years old before you can have a cash withdrawal card and, if you are under 18, some banks will ask for the permission of a parent or guardian before they will issue you with one.

Debit card

Debit cards are basically plastic cheque books that you can use to pay for goods and services. When you use a debit card, the details of the transaction are recorded electronically as the card is swiped through a terminal. The money is taken directly from your bank account.

Debit card for under 18s

You will normally have to be aged 18 before you can get a standard Switch or Delta debit card. If you are 11 or older, some banks will let you have a Solo or Electron card. This is a debit card where the balance in your account is checked before every transaction, so the payment only goes ahead if there is enough money in your account.

Credit card

You can use a credit card to buy things now and pay for them later. You can use credit cards to pay for goods and services as well as to withdraw cash. All credit cards have a maximum limit on the amount of money you can spend, called the credit limit. Credit cards are not usually available to people aged under 18. You can learn more about credit cards in Chapter 12.

Getting a credit card

Before getting credit you will normally have to complete an application form like the one below.

Credit Agreement regulated by the Consumer Credit Act 1974

About you

Name _____

Permanent Address _____

_____ Postcode _____

Number of years at
current address _____ years _____ months

Date of Birth _____ Place of birth _____

Are you: single ☐ married ☐ divorced ☐ widowed ☐ seperated ☐

Are you: home owner ☐ tenant ☐ living with parents ☐ other ☐

Your work and income

Are you: employed ☐ unemployed ☐ self-employed ☐ recieving a pension ☐
  student ☐ other ☐

Occupation _____

Net monthly income £ _____

Other monthly household income £ _____

Your Bank/Building Society details

Do you have a credit card? _____ Do you have a cheque card? _____

Do you have a
bank or savings Yes ☐ No ☐
account?

Name of bank/building society
_____

Time with bank/
building society _____ years

Our requirements

Name (BLOCK CAPITALS) _____

Signature _____

Date _____

What do you know?

1 Write down three advantages and disadvantages of using cards as opposed to cash.

2

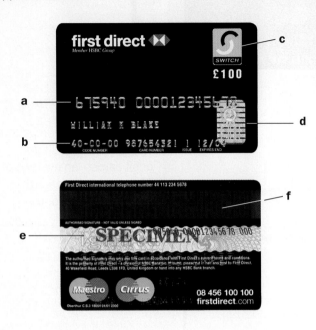

Make a copy of these cards.
Identify and write a brief comment about each of the areas (a to f) pointed to.

3 Design your own credit card. What information must you include on the credit card? Don't forget the other side of the card?

4 Make a list of shops that accept plastic cards. Which cards does each shop accept?
Make a list of shops that do not accept plastic cards. Why do you think this is?

5 Write an essay or a poem about a day in the life of a credit card.

6 Do you think we will still be using cash and cards in 2050? Give reasons for your answers.

12 Would you get credit?

What's all this about?

Consumer credit in the UK has increased by more than 60% in the last four years and is now running at £147 billion a year. Credit for goods and services can be obtained in many different ways but the most common include:

- hire purchase
- store cards
- personal loans
- credit cards
- overdrafts
- mail order catalogue.

Before considering whether to buy on credit, it is a good idea to weigh up the advantages and disadvantages of the various methods.

Type of credit	Advantages	Disadvantages
Hire purchase	It is convenient and allows you to pay for goods over a period of time.	An expensive way of borrowing. You do not own the goods until the last instalment has been paid.
Credit cards	Convenient, flexible and can provide you with interest-free credit if you pay off the outstanding balance each month.	An expensive way of borrowing in the long term if you do not pay off the outstanding balance each month.
Store card	Allows you to spread the cost of goods over a period of time and might also entitle you to special offers.	An expensive way of borrowing that can only be used in a certain number of stores.
Overdraft	Flexible way to borrow with no penalties for going overdrawn if you agree the arrangement with your bank in advance.	An expensive way of borrowing if the overdraft has not been agreed with your bank.
Personal loan	Allows you to plan your finances because you pay off the loan in fixed amounts at regular intervals.	Not very flexible, there is usually a charge if you pay off the loan early.
Mail order catalogue	It is convenient and allows you to pay for goods over a period of time.	Goods can be limited and may be slightly dearer than you would normally pay in a shop.

> What's the best way of borrowing money to buy things?

Would you believe it?

The word credit basically means giving someone time to pay. It comes from the Latin word 'credere' which means 'to believe'. When a retailer sells something to a customer, but gives them time to pay, they are trusting him or her to pay them back at a later date.

What does it mean?

Credit scoring

Most lenders use credit scoring to decide whether or not they will lend money to you. When you apply for a loan, you are asked various questions including your age, your employment, whether you own your own home and so on. The lender assigns you points, according to the answers you give. If your total score is above a certain limit, you qualify for a loan; if your score is less, you are likely to be turned down.

The 'Loans R Us' Finance Company uses credit scoring to help decide whether it will lend money to you. Here is a copy of their score card:

CONFIDENTIAL

Loans R Us Finance Company

CREDIT SCORE CARD

1. Age
   - Under 21 – score 0
   - 21-29 – score 1
   - 30-49 – score 4
   - 50-59 – score 2
   - 60 or more – score 1

2. Employment
   - Professional or skilled – score 4
   - Semi-skilled – score 2
   - Unskilled – score 1

3. Duration of employment
   - 3 years or more – score 4
   - 1 to 3 years – score 2
   - Under 1 year – score 1
   - Not employed – score 0

4. Home
   - Owner-occupied – score 4
   - Unfurnished tenant – score 2
   - Furnished tenant – score 1

5. Duration in current home
   - 3 years or more – score 4
   - 1 to 3 years – score 2
   - Under 1 year – score 0

6. Family
   - Married – score 4
   - Single/widowed – score 2
   - Divorced/separated – score 0

7. Children
   - No children – score 4
   - 1 child – score 1
   - 2 or more children – score 0

8. Bank account?
   - Yes – score 4
   - No – score 0

9. Income
   - £20,000 or more – score 4
   - £15,000 but less than £20,000 – score 2
   - £10,000 but less than £15,000 – score 1
   - Under £10,000 – score 0

Score 24 to 36: Grant loan

Score 0 to 23:   Refuse loan

Credit scoring can also be used 'on line' when you apply for a loan over the internet.

Use the score card to decide which of the following applicants will get their loan.

- Ahmad, 32, is married with two children. He has been a teacher for nine years and earns around £25 000 a year. He and his wife have lived in their current home for five years but are thinking of selling to buy somewhere bigger.
- Simon is 24 and shares a flat with his girlfriend, Mary, which they bought two years ago. He has been a trainee at a printing works for the last two years. Simon earns £12 000 a year. He is paid monthly by direct transfer into his bank account. Simon and Mary hope to get married next year and would like to start a family.
- Jenny, 19, is single and lives in bed and breakfast accommodation. She is not working at the moment because she is looking after her daughter, aged two. Her main source of income is state benefit, which is paid direct into her bank account.

Check your answers against those at the bottom of the page.

Credit reference agencies

A credit reference agency (CRA) is an organisation that gathers and stores information about individuals. The information includes:

- publicly available information, such as where you live and whether you have ever been taken to court for failing to pay your debts
- information from lenders about the amount you have borrowed from them and how well you have kept up the payments.

There are two main CRAs in the UK. They hold a credit file on nearly every adult in the country. You can get a copy of your credit file from a CRA for a small fee and you have the right to correct any errors that you find.

Who will be able to get loans?

Answers

Ahmad: scores 32 (if we assume he has a bank account, which is likely) so he is given the loan.

Simon: scores 19 so he is refused a loan.

Jenny: scores 9 to 10 depending on the amount she gets in state benefits and assuming that she is unskilled and has been in her current home less than a year. She is refused a loan.

What do you know?

1 Imagine that you need a loan of £15 000 to buy a car. Which of the following types of credit would be best?

- hire purchase
- store card
- personal loan
- credit card
- overdraft

Give reasons for your answers.

2 Design a credit scoring card of your own to decide whether a person should qualify for a loan.

Imagine that you will be lending them your own money, so you need to be very careful how you decide what makes someone creditworthy.

How does your credit scoring card compare with those of your friends? What areas do you agree are important? Why are they important?

3 Design a poster to explain what your rights are if you are refused credit. If for any reason you are refused credit you have the right:

- to know the name and address of the credit reference agency used
- to see any information held about you by that agency
- to correct any inaccurate information.

4 Carry out your own research on credit reference agencies.

Do you think that credit reference agencies are a good idea? Give reasons for your answers.

13 Buying without paying

What's all this about?

A popular way to buy goods without having to pay for them immediately is through hire purchase. Hire purchase is an agreement that lets you buy goods immediately while paying for them in instalments. Usually you do not own the goods until the last instalment is paid so if you do not pay an instalment then the goods can be taken back.

BUY NOW PAY LATER

This computer package can be yours for a small deposit and only £50 per month

The computer package is priced at £1000 and the small deposit is 10%, sounds too good to be true! But be careful, you do not know how long you will be paying that £50 per month, it could be one month, one year, ten years…

Always make sure you have all of the information before you decide to buy. Here is what the advert might have said…

BUY NOW PAY LATER

This computer package is normally £1000 and can be yours for a 10% deposit and 36 monthly payments of £50 per month.

… so now you can work out exactly what the hire purchase agreement is going to cost.

Work it out

Hire purchase costs

In order to work out how much the hire purchase agreement is going to cost, you will need to know the definitions below.

Cash price
What you pay for goods if you pay the whole price at the time you order the goods. It does not literally mean that you pay in cash however.

Total credit price
The total you must pay if you buy goods on credit. You find it by adding up the deposit, all the instalments and any other charges.

Hire purchase cost
The cost of buying goods on hire purchase. You can find the hire purchase cost using the total credit price and the cash price as follows:

hire purchase cost = total credit price − cash price

Now you can work out the hire purchase cost for the computer package.

How to find the hire purchase cost

BUY NOW PAY LATER

This computer package is normally £1000 and can be yours for a 10% deposit and 36 monthly payments of £50 per month.

The amount of the deposit = 10% of £1000
= £100

The total credit price = deposit + 36 monthly payments of £50
= £100 + (36 × £50)
= £100 + £1800
= £1900

The hire purchase cost = total credit price − cash price
= £1900 − £1000
= £900

Of course, 36 monthly payments of £50 may not seem like a lot of money but it can mean that you are paying a lot extra in order to spread your payments over three years. In this case you would pay an additional £900 for purchasing the computer package through hire purchase.

APR

Another useful way to compare borrowing is to use the **Annual Percentage Rate (APR)** which compares the cost of borrowing. It is expressed as so many per cent a year.

The APR takes into account:

- the rate of interest you must pay
- when and how often the interest must be paid
- other fees or charges (e.g. arrangement fees or annual membership fees)
- when and how often these fees and charges must be paid
- the cost of any compulsory credit insurance.

You do not need to know how to work out the APR. All you need to know is that a loan with a high APR is more expensive than one with a low APR.

Things to watch out for

Instant credit
Buy now, pay later schemes often look attractive, but you need to look carefully at the small print. You will usually get an interest-free period but after that you need to work out how much you will be paying. Remember to check the APR and compare it with other credit schemes or loans.

Furniture World...
... Exceptional savings!
Pay nothing for 1 whole year
(after deposit)

Interest-free credit
These schemes allow you to repay the amount you have borrowed over a period of time without charging you any interest. They may be tempting at first glance, but make sure that you cannot buy the goods cheaper elsewhere, and read the agreement's small print very carefully.

CARS 4 U
0%
Finance
APR over 2 years
See your dealer for more finance offers

What do you know?

1 A television set priced at £480 is offered for a deposit of £50 plus 24 monthly payments of £25. Find:

a) the total credit price,
b) the amount saved by paying cash.

2 A mountain bike is advertised at £450. It can also be bought on hire purchase for a deposit of £45 plus 12 monthly payments of £50. Find:

a) the total credit price,
b) the amount saved by paying cash.

3 The following table shows the monthly repayments for loans below £3000 over 12 months or 24 months, with and without the loan protection plan.

	Amount of loan	Monthly with loan protection	Monthly without loan protection
12 months	£50	£4.54	£4.54
	£100	£9.08	£9.08
	£500	£48.95	£45.32
	£1000	£97.88	£90.55
	£2000	£195.68	£181.22
24 months	£50	£2.42	£2.42
	£100	£5.36	£4.92
	£500	£26.85	£24.44
	£1000	£54.20	£48.80
	£2000	£108.85	£97.68

a) What is the total repayment on £500 over 12 months with the loan protection plan?
b) What is the total repayment on £1000 over 24 months without the loan protection plan?
c) What is the total repayment on £2000 over 12 months with the loan protection plan?
d) How much more is the loan protection plan on £100 over 24 months than the same loan without loan protection?

14 Unsure about insurance

What's all this about?

Although it is difficult to establish the exact history of insurance, we do know that a form of insurance existed in ancient Rome. Romans could contribute funds to a burial society so that when a member died the cost of burial was met by the society.

Merchants from Italy introduced marine insurance to Britain in the 13th century. As a result, it became common practice for merchants to give an assurance that if a loss occurred at sea then part of the cost would be recompensed.

During the 17th century, ships carrying valuable goods, such as spices and silks, were often lost or damaged by storms. For payment of a premium, some merchants would accept part of the risk. Many of these insurance and financial backing agreements were discussed in coffee houses, where ship owners and wealthy businessmen met. Lloyd's of London, which is still one of the best known names in insurance today, got its name from Edward Lloyd's 17th-century coffee house, near the Tower of London.

It is generally believed that fire insurance in Britain owes its origin to the Great Fire of London, which broke out in 1666. With that catastrophe in mind, a number of fire insurance projects were launched towards the end of the 17th century. Individual insurance companies began to form their own fire brigades. These brigades are thought to have been the first to operate in Britain since the Romans left, 1200 years earlier.

Plates, called fire marks, were placed in prominent positions on buildings that were insured against fire. These plates identified the insured properties in a time when only the principal streets were named and houses were not numbered.

What does it mean?

Insurance

Insurance pays out a sum of money if something bad happens to you. The aim of insurance is to compensate you so that you are no worse off, but no better off, than you were before.

The exception is life insurance (technically called 'life assurance') which pays out if the insured person dies. Life insurance pays out the sum agreed when the insurance was taken out.

Different types of insurance

Car insurance

Car insurance covers you if you injure or kill someone else or damage someone else's property (called 'third party insurance'). You can get additional cover according to which of the following policies you choose:

- **third party, fire and theft** provides only limited cover for the car including theft
- **comprehensive insurance** provides full cover including loss and damage.

You must, by law, have car insurance if you drive on public roads.

House insurance

There are two types of house insurance which cover the outside (including the structure) and the contents.

- **buildings insurance** pays out if the buildings are damaged or destroyed
- **contents insurance** pays out if the things inside your home are damaged or stolen.

All risks cover

An extension to house contents insurance, which you can take out to cover valuable items, such as jewellery, cameras and computers.

Holiday insurance

This pays out if disaster strikes when you go on holiday. For example, it covers the cancellation of your holiday because of illness, your luggage being lost or stolen, hospital treatment abroad, being flown back home if you are taken ill and so on.

Health insurance

There are several different types of health insurance including:

- **private medical insurance** pays out if you have to go into hospital for any reason (sometimes subject to conditions)
- **income protection insurance** replaces part of your wages or salary if you can't work because you are ill
- **critical illness insurance** pays out a cash sum if you are diagnosed with a life-threatening condition, such as cancer or heart disease
- **long-term care insurance** pays the cost of being looked after at home or the cost of nursing home care if you become too ill or disabled to look after yourself.

Would you believe it?

And finally, here are some excuses provided to insurance companies by people making claims.

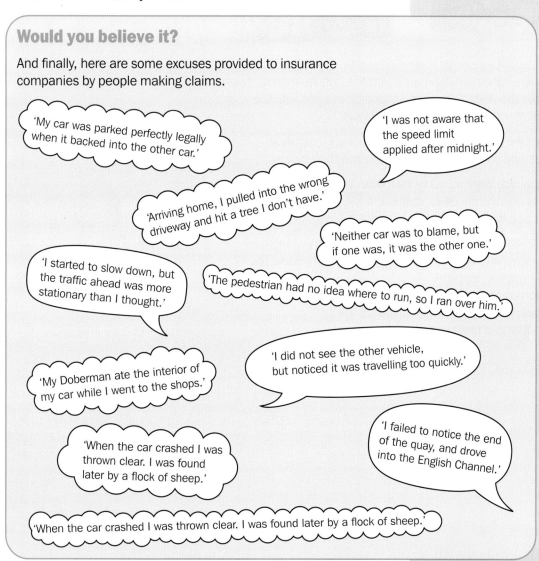

'My car was parked perfectly legally when it backed into the other car.'

'I was not aware that the speed limit applied after midnight.'

'Arriving home, I pulled into the wrong driveway and hit a tree I don't have.'

'Neither car was to blame, but if one was, it was the other one.'

'I started to slow down, but the traffic ahead was more stationary than I thought.'

'The pedestrian had no idea where to run, so I ran over him.'

'My Doberman ate the interior of my car while I went to the shops.'

'I did not see the other vehicle, but noticed it was travelling too quickly.'

'When the car crashed I was thrown clear. I was found later by a flock of sheep.'

'I failed to notice the end of the quay, and drove into the English Channel.'

'When the car crashed I was thrown clear. I was found later by a flock of sheep.'

What do you know?

The emblems shown belong to the London Assurance and the Royal Exchange Assurance which were granted Royal Charters in 1720 to transact marine insurance.

The London Assurance amalgamated with the Sun Alliance Company in 1965, while the Royal Exchange Assurance merged with the Guardian Insurance Company Limited in 1968.

1 Write down the names of some of the other big insurance companies and carry out some research into their history.

2 Imagine that you want to insure your bike. Undertake some research to find the cheapest quote and the most expensive quote. You might also want to complete a proposal form to insure your chosen item.

3 If you managed an insurance company, how much would you charge to insure a computer?
How did you come to your decision?
What sort of questions would you need to ask?
Don't forget to give reasons for your questions.

15 Holiday money

What's all this about?

One of the fun things about going abroad is dealing with foreign currency and trying to work out the cost of goods and services. As foreign travel becomes more commonplace, so our need to understand different currencies becomes increasingly important.

Try out the quiz below to test your knowledge of foreign currency. You can find information on exchange rates in newspapers and banks.

Quiztime

Easy Quiz

1 How many pence in £1?
2 In which country would you spend a rand?
3 Complete the following:
    100 kopeks = ...
4 What is the currency of Israel called?
5 Where would you see this currency?

6 Would you rather have £100 or $100?

Hard Quiz

1 How many cents in $1?
2 In which country would you spend a won?
3 Complete the following:
    100 centaros = ...
4 What is the currency of Venezuela called?
5 Where would you see this currency?

6 Would you rather have £100 or €100?

Your score:

0–2 A holiday in Eastbourne might be a better holiday destination for you!
3–4 You will need to keep a careful eye on your money when you go abroad.
5–6 You will manage well abroad and shouldn't find foreign currency that foreign.

Answers

Easy Quiz
1 100 pence in £1
2 South Africa
3 100 kopeks = 1 rouble
4 Shekel
5 Japan
6 £100

Hard Quiz
1 100 cents in $1
2 Korea
3 100 centaros = 1 real
4 Bolivar
5 Denmark
6 £100

The euro

It is not always necessary to exchange money when travelling across Europe. Twelve of the countries belonging to the European Union (including France and Germany, but not the UK so far) have agreed to replace their national currencies with a new single, common currency called the euro.

Work it out

£1 =

1.4 American dollars	2.3 Swiss francs
1.6 European euro	6.1 Egyptian pounds
175 Japanese yen	08.6 Indian rupees

Which of the currencies below is worth the most money in pounds?

America	Japan	Russia
140 dollars	175 yen	422 roubles

To convert currency into pounds, you divide the amount by the exchange rate.

currency	exchange rate	currency ÷ exchange rate	
140 dollars	1.4	140 ÷ 1.4	= £100
175 yen	175	175 ÷ 175	= £1
422 roubles	42.2	422 ÷ 42.2	= £10

America	Japan	Russia
140 dollars = £100	175 yen = £1	422 roubles = £10

So the American dollars are worth the most money in pounds.

The twelve countries are: Belgium, Germany, Greece, Spain, France, Ireland, Italy, Luxembourg, The Netherlands, Austria, Portugal and Finland. Greece joined the original eleven in January 2001.

The front of each euro coin has a common design for all twelve countries, but the reverse side displays different designs for each country.

Who wants to be a millionaire?

In Romania, at the time of writing, the exchange rate was:

44 182 leu = £1

If	£1	= 44 182 leu
then	£23	= 23 × 44 182 leu
		= 1 016 186 leu (that is over **one million** leu!)

So, in Romania, you could be a millionaire for just £23!
How much would you need to be a millionaire in other countries?

What does it mean?

Exchange rate
The amount of foreign currency you'll get in exchange for £1, for example, the number of dollars you'll get for £1.

Bureau de change
A shop, or counter where money can be exchanged for other currencies. You will find these in banks, post offices, travel agents and at airports, ferry terminals etc.

Commission
Commission is the fee charged by the bank (or other financial institution) for converting your money from one currency to another. Some institutions charge higher rates of commission than others so it is best to shop around.

Would you believe it?

The phrase 'bureau de change' is French for 'exchange office'. The plural is 'bureaux de change'.

What do you know?

1 Work these out using the exchange rates listed on page 58.

a) How many Swiss francs will you get for £20?
b) How much is £686 pounds in rupees?
c) How many Polish zloty will you get for £155?
d) How much are 6390 baht worth in English pounds?
e) How much are 32 euros worth in English pounds?

2 Find out the name of the currency for the following countries:

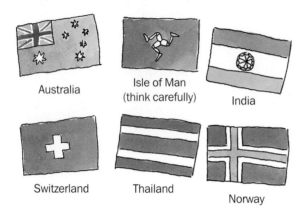

Australia

Isle of Man
(think carefully)

India

Switzerland

Thailand

Norway

What is the exchange rate for these countries?

3 The pictures below show the reverse sides of the euro for six different countries.
Can you guess which countries they are from?
What can you find out about the origin of these designs?

4 Create your own design for a new euro coin to replace the pound. What distinctive features would you wish to include on the coin? What about coins for Scotland, Wales and Northern Ireland?

5 Write down some advantages and disadvantages of having a common currency across Europe. What about some advantages and disadvantages of having a common currency across the world?

Glossary

APR

Annual percentage rate (APR) is the cost of borrowing or buying on credit expressed as 'so many per cent a year'.

The APR takes into account such things as: the rate of interest you must pay

- when and how often the interest must be paid,
- other fees or charges (e.g. arrangement fees or annual membership fees),
- when and how often these fees and charges must be paid,
- the cost of any credit insurance that is part of the deal.

You do not need to know how to work out the APR. All you need to know is that a loan with a high APR is more expensive than one with a low APR.

Bank accounts

There are many different accounts and some of them have very unusual names but the most common types of account are current accounts and savings accounts.
(see also Current account and Saving account)

Banks

Banks are companies whose business is handling people's money. They provide a variety of services to depositors (for example bank accounts) and borrowers (for example loans).

Banks are owned by shareholders so that any profits made are given back to the shareholders.
(see also Building societies and Credit unions)

Building societies

Building societies are organisations whose business is handling people's money. They provide a variety of services to depositors (for example savings facilities) and borrowers (for example loans for house purchases etc.). Building societies are owned by the customers so that any profits made belong to them.
(see also Banks and Credit unions)

Bureau de change

A shop or counter where money can be exchanged for other currencies. You'll find these in banks, post offices, travel agents or else at airports, ferry terminals etc.
NB The word 'Bureau de change' is French for 'exchange office' and the plural is 'bureaux de change'.

Cash withdrawal card

Cash cards are cards issued by banks and building societies to allow the owner to withdraw money from a cash dispenser or else check your balance and sometimes get statements from an ATM.

You will usually have to be aged 11 before you can have a cash withdrawal card and, if you are under 18, some banks will ask for the permission of a parent or guardian before they will issue one to you.

Cheque book/Cheques

Once you're 18, your bank may issue you with a book of cheques which you complete when paying for goods or services. You need to write the name of the person you want to pay (the payee), the amount of money in words and in figures, the date and your signature.

The person receiving the cheque can pay it into their bank and the money will be transferred from your account to theirs - this process usually takes about three days.

Cheque guarantee cards

Cheque guarantee cards are cards that guarantee a cheque up to a particular value (usually £50 or £100). By writing your cheque guarantee card number on the back of the cheque, the retailer will be paid even if there is not enough money in your account to honour the cheque you've written.

A cheque guarantee card will usually only be available if you are over 18 and have a regular income.

Commission

Commission is the fee paid by the bank (or other financial institution) for converting your money from one currency to another.

NB Some institutions charge higher rates of commission than others so it is best to shop around

Credit

A credit is any payment of money into a bank account – for example, when you pay in cash or a cheque or your employer automatically transfers your wages to your account using BACS.

Credit card

You can use credit cards to pay for goods and services as well as to withdraw cash. All credit cards have a maximum limit on the amount of money you can spend and this is called the credit limit. Different people have different credit limits depending upon their circumstances.

Each month you receive a statement which tells you what you have spent, what you have paid and what you owe. You can pay back any amount from the minimum amount shown to the full amount outstanding. If you do not pay off the outstanding balance by the date shown on your statement then you will be charged interest until it is paid in full.

Credit cards are not usually available to people aged under 18.

Credit insurance

Credit insurance is also called 'loan protection insurance' or 'payment protection insurance' and is an insurance which makes your loan repayments for you if you become unemployed or can't work because of illness.

Credit scoring

Lenders use credit scoring to decide whether or not they will lend to you. When you apply for a loan, you are asked various questions about, for example, your age, your employment, whether you own your own home and so on. The lender assigns you points according to the answers you give. If your total score is above a certain limit, you qualify for a loan; if your score is less, you are likely to be turned down.

Each lender has its own credit scoring system so, even if you are turned down by one lender, you might be accepted by another. Credit scoring systems are commercially sensitive information that lenders keep secret. If you are turned down for a loan, the lender will not tell you your score. However, if you ask, the lender should give you some broad indication of the reason for being turned down.

Credit unions

Credit unions, which are very popular in the USA, Canada and Ireland are organisations which provide savings facilities for depositors and loans for borrowers. The members must share some common bond, such as working for the same employer, living in the same area, or belonging to the same church.
(see also Banks and Building societies)

Credit reference agencies

A credit reference agency (CRA) is an organisation which gathers and stores information about individuals. It then sells that information to lenders to help them work out the risk of lending to a person. The information is of two types:

- Publicly available information, such as where you live (taken from the electoral roll) and whether you have any county court judgements against you (because you have been taken to court for failing to pay your debts)
- Information from lenders about the amount you've borrowed from them and how well you've kept up the payments. Only lenders who have agreed to provide the CRA with this type of information about their customers can access this type of information about other people.

There are two main CRAs in the UK. They hold a credit file on nearly every adult in the country. You can get a copy of your own credit file from a CRA for a small fee and you have the right to correct any errors.

Current account

A current account can be used to pay in wages, salaries and any other money you receive. A current account keeps your money safe and helps you manage your day-to-day finances.

It offers various ways to pay for the things you buy without having to use cash for example a debit card, cheque book, direct debits and standing orders. You will receive a regular bank statement to show you how much has been paid in and drawn out.

Debit

A debit is any payment of money out of your bank account – for example, when you withdraw cash at an ATM, write someone a cheque or make a payment by direct debit.

Debit card

Debit cards are basically plastic cheque books which you can use to pay for goods and services. Debit cards allow you to pay for goods and services using the money in your bank account. When you use a debit card the details are recorded electronically as the card is swiped through a terminal and the money is taken directly from your bank account.

You will have to be aged 18 before you can get a standard Switch or Delta card, but from the age of 11 some banks will let you have a Solo or Electron card. These cards are special debit cards which stop you from taking more money out of your account than you actually have.

Euro

Eleven of the countries in the European Union (but not the UK – so far) have agreed that they will replace their national currencies with a new single, common currency from 1 January 2002. The new European currency is called the Euro and, in future, you will exchange your pounds for Euros instead of buying marks when you visit Germany or francs when you visit France .

Exchange rate

The amount of foreign currency you'll get in exchange for £1, for example, the number of dollars you'll get for £1.

Hire purchase

Hire Purchase is an agreement which lets you use goods immediately while paying for them in instalments. Usually, you do not own the goods until the last instalment is paid so if you don't pay then the goods can be taken back.

Hourly pay

Hourly pay is the amount of money that is paid for each hour of work usually for an agreed number of hours each week.

Income tax

This is a tax due on most types of income, including earnings from a job. Everyone has a personal allowance, which means that your first slice of income is tax-free. Income above this amount is taxed according to a formula which means that the greater your earnings then the bigger your tax bill.

Mail order

Mail order is where you choose goods from a published catalogue (or website). You can choose to pay the full price of the goods when you order them or you can by on credit, thus spreading the payment over a number of weeks or months.

National insurance contributions

National Insurance (NI) is a tax that the government uses to pay for state pensions and other state benefits, such as those paid to people who are too ill to work..

Overdraft

An overdraft is a negative bank balance – in other words, a balance where you have spent more than you put in. If you agree the overdraft in advance with your bank manager, you pay interest on what you borrow and perhaps an arrangement fee or a flat-rate fee. If you do not arrange the overdraft in advance, then there are usually hefty extra charges.

Overtime

Overtime is money paid for working more than the agreed number of hours each week. Overtime is often paid at a different rate such as 'time and a half' which means $1\frac{1}{2}$ times the normal rate or 'double time' which means 2 times the normal rate.

PAYE

PAYE stands for 'Pay As You Earn'. PAYE is operated by your employer who deducts income tax and National Insurance from your earnings and then pays these direct to the government.

Pension contributions

The pensions paid by the state are very low, so many people build up an extra pension for payment on retirement. If you pay into a pension scheme or plan organised by an employer, your contributions are deducted from your earnings.

Personal loans

A personal loan is an arrangement to borrow a set amount of money for a fixed period of time (the 'term'). You agree to make fixed payments every month which repay the sum you borrowed and cover interest charged on it.

If you want to pay off the loan early, you'll usually have to pay an 'early redemption fee' to compensate the lender for at least part of the interest which it would have earned had you kept on paying for the full term.

Personal Identification Number (PIN)

In order to withdraw money from an ATM a customer needs a card issued by the appropriate bank or building society and the correct Personal Identification Number (PIN).

The PIN is a four digit number which you can consider to be your own password - the PIN is entirely private to the cardholder and it is very important that you do not tell anyone else your PIN and that you do not write it down.

Purse card

These are plastic cards you load with money (taken from your bank account, say, or in exchange for cash) and then use to pay for things. Some purse cards let you pay for only one type of purchase – for example, telephone calls or meals in a school canteen.

Other cards – such as Mondex which was trialed in Swindon are designed to be used in a wide range of outlets just like debit and credit cards. If you lose the card, you also lose the money on it in the same way that, if you lost your purse, you'd lose the cash in it.

Salary

A salary is the amount of money paid for a job and generally dependent upon the number of hours worked and the rate of pay.

NB The word 'salary' comes from the Latin 'sal'

meaning salt and harks back to the days when Romans were paid in salt.

(see also Wages)

Savings account

A savings account pays you interest on the amount you have saved and allows you to put money aside for the future. You can use a savings account to save regularly or pay into it when you have some spare cash.

There are different types of savings accounts depending on whether you have a lump sum to invest or smaller amounts and how quickly you may want to draw your money out.

Statement

A statement is a record of the payments you have made into your account, the amounts you have drawn out and the balance left. Through an ATM, you can often get a statement showing, say, the last ten transactions. Most banks and building societies will also regularly send you a statement through the post.

Tax allowance

Everyone – even a child – is given a personal allowance which is the amount of income which you can earn before you start having to pay tax.

Tax bands

Your taxable income is divided into slices called 'bands'. Tax on the first slice is charged at a fairly low rate. The next slice is charged at a higher rate and the top slice is charged at the highest rate of all. This arrangement is a way of ensuring that poorer people lose less of their income in tax than richer people.

Taxable income

Taxable income is the amount of income on which income tax is to be paid. The amount of taxable income is found by subtracting allowances from the annual income.

Taxable income = income − allowances

Tax rates

The tax rate tells you how much tax you must pay on your income. The rate is expressed as a percentage. For example, a tax rate of 10% means that you will pay 10p tax for every £1 you get and a tax rate of

22% means that you will pay 22p tax for every £1 you get .

Tax relief

The government gives tax relief to encourage you to spend money on certain things, such as saving for a pension or giving to charity.

For example, if you wish to give £10 to charity (using a scheme called Gift Aid) then you can give £7.80 to the charity and the charity can claim a further £2.20 from the government. So the charity gets £10 but you pay only £7.80. and the difference (£10 - £7.80 = £2.20) is your tax relief.

Total credit price

This means the total you must pay for any goods which you buy on credit. You find it by adding up the deposit, all the instalments and any other charges. Usually the total comes to more than you would pay if you paid the full price of the goods when you ordered them.

Travellers cheques

These are special cheques which you buy from your bank at home. When you sign them and hand them to a bank abroad, they will give you the value of the cheque in foreign money.

You can also use travellers' cheques to pay for things in a shop, restaurant, hotel and so on just as you would use a normal cheque at home. If your travellers cheques are lost or stolen, then a refund can be arranged.

Wages

A wage is the amount of money paid for a job and is usually dependent upon the number of hours worked and the rate of pay.

(see also Salary)

Index

Acknowledgements

The publishers thank the following for permission to reproduce copyright material:

Corbis, pp. 2, 53; Corel (NT), pp.16, 20, 58 left, middle and right; E.V. Jackson Reproductions, Canada, p. 56; HSBC Group, pp. 42 lower, middle and bottom, 43, 44 top and bottom; Mary Evans Picture Library, pp. 21, 28 top (unnamed artist in the Ellesmere manuscript of the Canterbury Tales reproduced in Green's History), 28 bottom (after Alexander Nasmyth, 1787, reproduced on a postcard); NatWest Bank plc, p. 42 top.

The publishers have made every effort to contact copyright holders but apologise if any have been overlooked.